snapshot·picture·library

CATS

snapshot·picture·library

CATS

FOG CITY PRESS

Published by Fog City Press,
a division of Weldon Owen Inc.
415 Jackson Street
San Francisco, CA 94111 USA
www.weldonowen.com

WELDON OWEN INC.
Group Publisher, Bonnier Publishing Group John Owen
Chief Executive Officer and President Terry Newell
Senior Vice President, International Sales Stuart Laurence
Vice President, Sales and New Business Development Amy Kaneko
Vice President, Publisher Roger Shaw
Vice President, Creative Director Gaye Allen
Managing Editor, Fog City Press Karen Perez
Assistant Editor Sonia Vallabh
Art Director Bret Hansen
Designer Andreas Schueller
Design Assistant Kevin Yuen
Production Director Chris Hemesath
Production Manager Michelle Duggan
Color Manager Teri Bell

Text Barbara Vivian Rogers and Albert Wollmer
Picture Research Brandi Valenza

A WELDON OWEN PRODUCTION
© 2008 Weldon Owen Inc.

Library of Congress Control Number: 2008926989

ISBN-13: 978-1-74089-993-2

10 9 8 7 6 5 4 3 2 1
2009   2010   2011   2012

Printed by Tien Wah Press in Singapore.

Look, a calico cat is walking across your rooftop! Its steps sound like the pitter-patter of raindrops. It leaps down and walks over to you, hoping that you'll rub its furry belly and scratch behind its ears.

You may see cats every day. Cats playing. Cats sleeping. Cats running. Cats purring. But what you may not see is the world of a cat: a world filled with exploration, wonder, and many, many naps.

Have you ever seen
a cat prowling
in a field, looking
for mice and
birds to eat?

Or maybe you
have seen a
cat slinking
across the city.

Cats live in nearly every
environment on Earth—sunny
places and snowy places.

Cats are alert
even when they lie
about. They always
want to know
what's going on.

Cats can often be found snooping around for a new adventure.

Playing with toys is another way cats explore their world. Cat toys can be as simple as a piece of ribbon, a feather, or a jingly ball.

Exploration can lead to many new discoveries, like finding running water or a big puddle!

Cats have a unique
way of looking
at the world. But
just like us, cats
enjoy stretching
out to soak up the
warmth of the sun.

Or looking
closely at the
world as it
goes by.

Cats like to roll on their backs,
warm their bellies, and have a
good scratch, too.

Cats like to find tight places to squeeze into... like a paper bag, a doorway, or a pile of rocks. Places like these make them feel secure and safe.

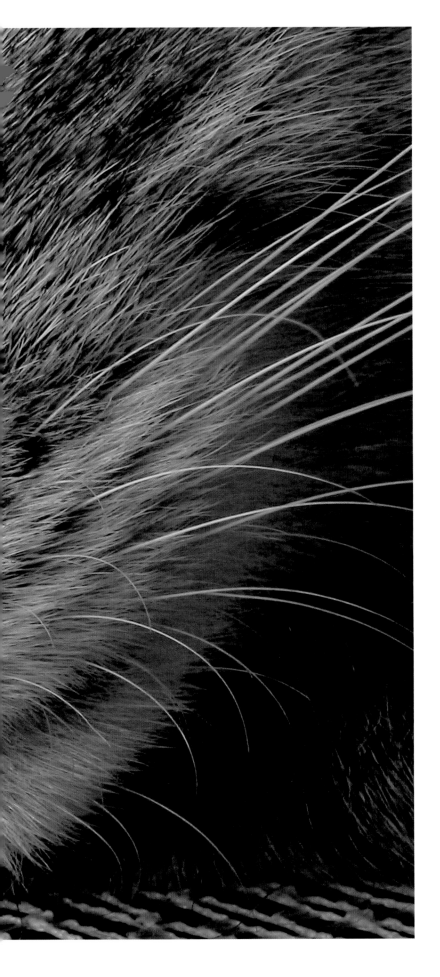

Once a cat finds
a safe, secure
spot, it's usually
a perfect time
for a nap!

But cats can snooze anywhere
they can lay their tails...

...such as on a bench, curled up.

In between naps, cats enjoy pouncing and playing with their furry friends.

Cats can truly
be perfect pals.

If you touch a cat's tongue, you'll
find it feels rough, like sandpaper.

You might see a cat's bright red tongue playfully poking out when it meows or yawns.

A cat's tongue
makes a perfect
washcloth
when it needs
to take a bath.

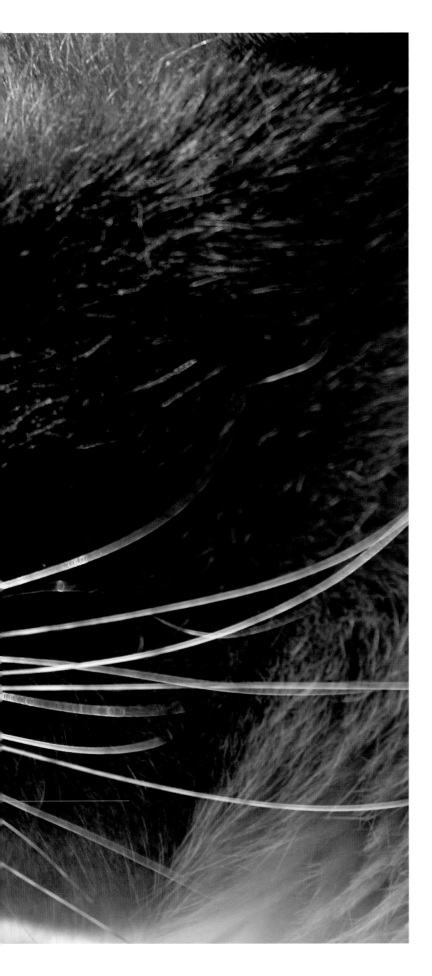

Cats have tiny noses that are surrounded by wiry whiskers.

Some cats have long, soft coats that are pleasant to pet.

Cats can come with spots and stripes, no hair, or markings called *points*.

Cats have colorful, jewel-like eyes. Their eyes can be blue, green, yellow, brown—even red or orange.

Padded paws are perfect for
playing, but watch out—cats
can also have sharp claws!

No matter where they are, cats
can find a comfortable perch.

And cats can be elegant and
graceful—most of the time!

The world of
a cat is full of
wonderful friends,
adventures, and
naps. Do you think
that you would
like to be a cat?

Blue Tabby Longhair

 Blue Tabby and White Shorthair

 Bicolor Shorthair

 Russian Blue Longhair

 Turkish Van Red Shorthair

 Mitted Red Tabby Shorthair

 Calico Longhair

 Blue Tabby Shorthair

 Tortoiseshell Shorthair

 Red Tabby Shorthair

 Blue Tabby Longhair

 Brown Tabby Shorthair

 Black Shorthair

 Red Mackerel Tabby and White Shorthair

 Mackerel Tabby

 Siamese

 Blue Patched Tabby Point Longhair

 Tuxedo Shorthair

 Brown Tabby Shorthair

 Torbie and White Shorthair

 Chocolate Bicolor

 Red Tabby Piebald Shorthair

 Blue Tabby Shorthair

 Cream Burmese

 Torbie and White Shorthair

 Brown Tabby Shorthair

 Tuxedo Shorthair

 Seal Point Traditional Siamese

 Turkish Van Shorthair

 Red Tabby Shorthair

Torbie Shorthair

 Brown Tabby and White Shorthair

 Silver Tabby Longhair

 Red Tabby Shorthair and Calico Shorthair

 Chocolate Burmese

 Calico Shorthair

 Van Blue Tabby Shorthair and Red Tabby Shorthair

 Blue Tabby Longhair

 Bicolor British Shorthair

 Red Tabby Piebald Shorthair and Brown Tabby Shorthair

 Brown Tabby Longhair

 Classical Siamese

 Blue Point Ragdoll

 Tortoiseshell Longhair

 Tuxedo Shorthair

 White Persian

 Bengal

 White Shorthair

 Red Tabby Piebald Shorthair

 Solid Black Sphynx

 Brown Tabby Shorthair

 Brown Tabby Shorthair

 Seal Point Siamese

 Mackerel Tabby Longhair

 Cream Tabby Shorthair

 Silver Tabby Piebald Shorthair

ACKNOWLEDGMENTS

Weldon Owen would like to thank the following people for their assistance in the production of this book: Lori Cockerill, Lucie Parker, Phil Paulick, and Heather Stewart.

CREDITS

All images courtesy of Shutterstock, except the cover courtesy of iStockphoto and page 45 bottom courtesy of Dreamstime.